READING/WRITING COMPANION

McGraw Hill Education

Cover: Nathan Love, Erwin Madrid

mheducation.com/prek-12

Send all inquiries to:
McGraw-Hill Education
Two Penn Plaza
New York, NY 10121

ISBN: 978-0-07-901784-0
MHID: 0-07-901784-3

Printed in the United States of America.

9 LMN 23 22   D

Welcome to Wonders!

Explore exciting **Literature**, **Science**, and **Social Studies** texts!

★ **READ** about the world around you!

★ **THINK**, **SPEAK**, and **WRITE** about genres!

★ **COLLABORATE** in discussions and inquiry!

★ **EXPRESS** yourself!

my.mheducation.com

Use your student login to read texts and practice phonics, spelling, grammar, and more!

Unit 3 Going Places

The Big Idea

Week 1 • Rules to Go By

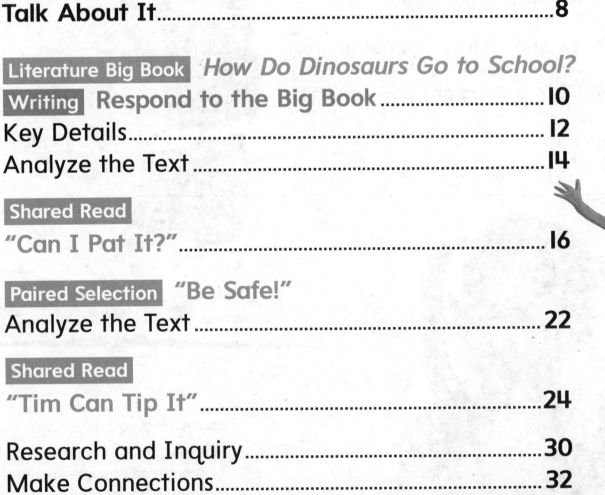

 Digital Tools Find this eBook and other resources at: my.mheducation.com

Week 2 • Sounds Around Us

Week 3 • The Places We Go

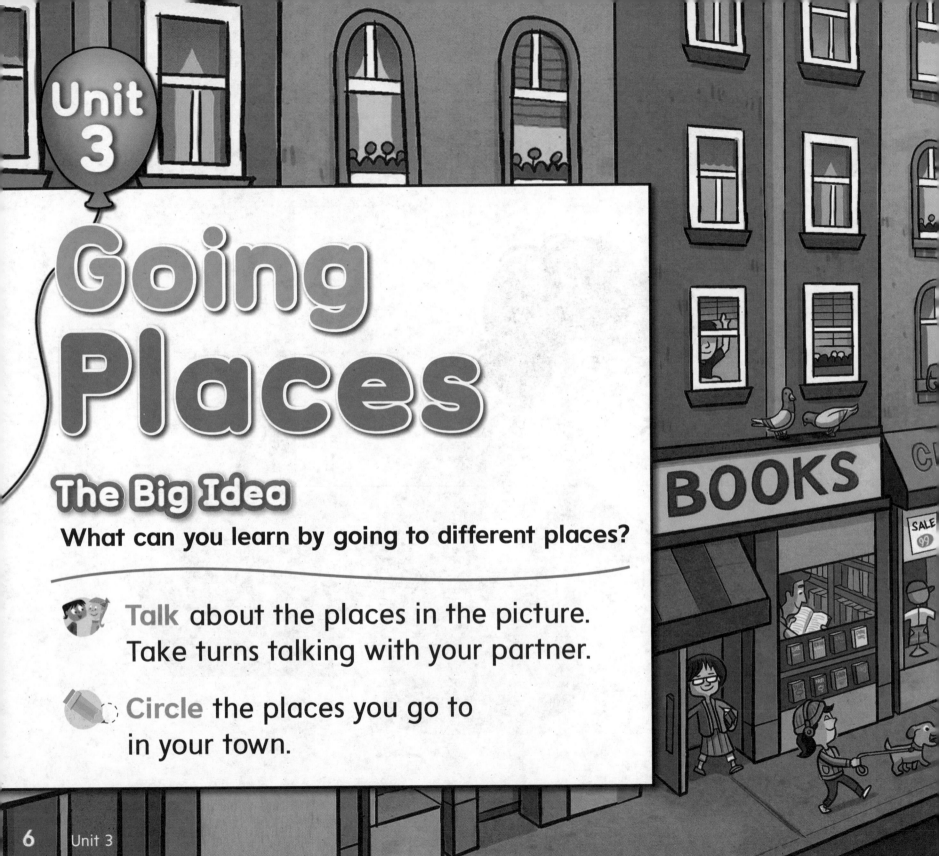

Unit 3

Going Places

The Big Idea

What can you learn by going to different places?

Talk about the places in the picture. Take turns talking with your partner.

Circle the places you go to in your town.

Talk About It

Essential Question What rules do we follow in different places?

Talk about the game these children are playing.

 Draw yourself playing a game.

 Write about a rule in the game.

A rule is

_____

- -

_____

Retell the story.

 Write about the story.

A funny part of the story is

_____

- -

_____

 Text Evidence

Page

A part that was not funny is

_____

- -

_____

 Text Evidence

Page

- -

_____

Talk about rules you follow at school.

 Draw and **write** about a rule you follow at school.

The rule is

_____

- -

_____

Key details tell important information that helps you understand the story.

 Listen to part of the story.

 Talk about key details.

 Write two key details.

Two key details are

_____

1. _____

_____

2. _____

Draw one detail you wrote about.

 Talk about why the detail is important.

Look at pages 14–21.

 Talk about how the dinosaurs act in school.

 Draw one way the dinosaurs act.

Listen to pages 24–29.

 Talk about how the dinosaurs act in school. How have they changed?

 Draw one way the dinosaurs act.

 **Make Inferences**

The author tells the story in two parts. She organizes the text this way to show how the dinosaurs change. How is the first part different from the second part? What does the author want you to know about how the dinosaurs should act?

Find Text Evidence

Read to find out what the girl can pat.

Circle the word to.

Can I Pat It?

I like to pat it.

Find Text Evidence

Underline the uppercase letters.

Circle what the girl can pat on page 19.

Can I pat it?

I like to pat it.

Shared Read

 Find Text Evidence

Circle an animal whose name has the same middle sound as **pin**.

Retell the story. Tell what happens in order.

I like it.

Can I pat it?

Look at the photo. How can we stay safe when riding a bike?

Talk about ways the boy stays safe on the bike.

Circle ways the boy stays safe.

Quick Tip

We can talk about staying safe using these words:

We can stay safe by ___.

It is dangerous to ___.

Listen to the "Biking Rules" list.

 Draw another way you can stay safe on a bike.

 Write the new rule.

Talk About It

How does the author share information about safety?

Read to find out what Tim can tip.

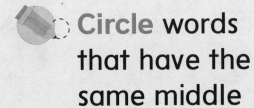 **Circle** words that have the same middle sound as **sit**.

Tim Can Tip It

Tim can tip the .

pail

Shared Read

Find Text Evidence

 Circle the word that tells what Tim does with the bag. Use the picture to help you.

Read and point to each word in the sentence on page 27.

Tim can tip the .

bag

Tim can see the tap.
bird

Find Text Evidence

 Circle the word on page 29 that tells what Tim does to the cat.

Retell the story. Use the words and pictures to help you.

Tim can see the  tap.

cat

Tim can sit to pat the .
cat

Rules for Safety

Step 1 **Talk** about rules we follow for safety.

Step 2 **Write** a question about how to stay safe at home or school.

_____

- -

_____

_____

- -

_____

Step 3 **Look** at books or use the Internet.

Step 4 **Draw** and **write** about what you learned.

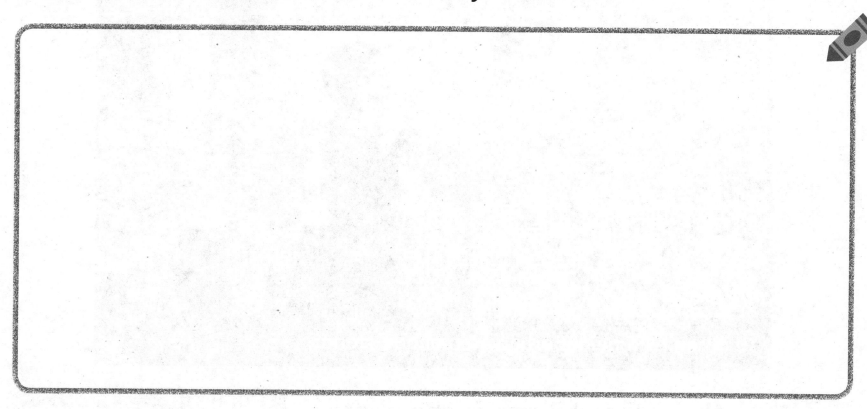

I can stay safe by

_____

- - - - - - - - - - - - - - - - - - - -

_____

Step 5 **Choose** a good way to present your work.

Children at a neighborhood lemonade stand.

 Talk about the children in the photo. What rule are they following?

 Compare these children to the dinosaurs at the end of *How Do Dinosaurs Go to School?*

Rosemarie Gearhart/E+/Getty Images

Quick Tip

To talk about rules, we can say:

A rule we follow is ___.

This rule is important because ___.

What I Know Now

Think about the texts you read this week.

The texts tell about

_____

- -

_____

- -

_____

 Think about what you learned this week.
What else would you like to learn?
Talk about your ideas.

 Share one thing you learned
about fiction stories.

Talk About It

? Essential Question What are the different sounds we hear?

Talk about the sounds these musical instruments make.

Draw and **write** about yourself playing a musical instrument.

I am playing a

_____

- -

_____

Retell the story.

 Write about the story.

A sound the boy hears is

_____

- -

_____

Text Evidence

Page

My favorite sound in the story is

_____

- -

_____

 Text Evidence

Page

- -

_____

Talk about things that make sounds in your neighborhood.

 Draw something that makes a sound.

 Write a sound word for your drawing.

Key details tell important information that helps you understand the story.

 Listen to part of the story.

 Talk about the key details.

 Write two key details.

Two key details are

1. _____

2. _____

Draw the two details you wrote about.

1.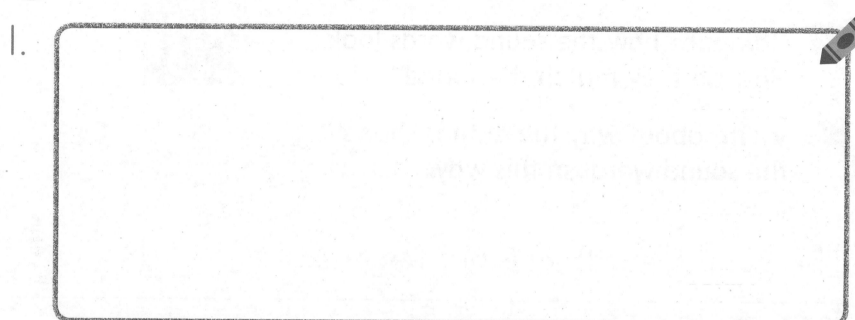

2.

Look at pages 20–21 and 26–27.

 Compare how the sound words look. How do they match the sound?

 Write about why the author shows the sound words in this way.

The sound words are big because

_____

- -

_____

The sound words are little because

_____

- -

_____

Listen to pages 30–31.

 Draw who is making the sounds on these pages.

 Talk about how you know.

Find Text Evidence

Read to find out about Nat and Tip.

Circle words that begin with the same sound as **nap**.

Nat and Tip

Nat and Tip like the ⬤.
ball

Shared Read

🔍 **Find Text Evidence**

✏️ **Underline** words that rhyme on page 44.

✏️ **Circle** who Nat and Tip see on page 45.

Nat and Tip like to sip.

Nat and Tip see the  .

children

Find Text Evidence

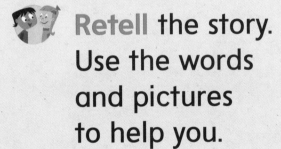

Circle the word **and**.

Retell the story. Use the words and pictures to help you.

Nat and Tip 👂 the 🔨.

hear   hammer

Nat and Tip  the !

hear   dog

Look at the photos. How do musical instruments make sounds?

Air makes the trumpet vibrate.

 Circle this musical instrument.

 Draw lines to show sounds coming out of the instrument.

Quick Tip

To **vibrate** means to move back and forth quickly.

Talk about this photo and caption.

 Write what the caption tells about the photo.

Talk About It

How do the photos show ways sounds are being made? What information do the captions add?

Hands beat on the drum and make the drum vibrate.

The caption tells about

_____

- -

_____

🔍 **Find Text Evidence**

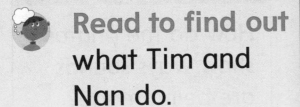

Read to find out what Tim and Nan do.

✏️ **Circle** a word that begins with the same sound as **nap**.

Tim and Nan

Tim and Nan the 🐔 .
hear   hen

Circle an object whose name ends with the same sound as **sun**.

Underline the word **and**.

Tim and Nan 👂 the 🚜.

hear   tractor

Tim and Nan see the .

corn

Shared Read

 Find Text Evidence

 Circle what Tim and Nan see on page 54.

 Retell the text. Use the words and photos to help you.

Tim and Nan see the barn.

Tim and Nan the .

hear pig

Research Sounds

Step 1 Talk about objects that you might use to make sounds. Choose some to try.

Step 2 Write a question about sounds you might make with your objects.

_____

- -

_____

_____

- -

_____

Step 3 Experiment with your objects. Try different ways to make sounds.

Step 4 Draw how you made sounds
with your objects. Label your picture
with a sound word.

Step 5 Choose a good way to present your work.

What Does the Rain Say?

What does the rain say?
Drip, Drop, Drip!
What does the chick say?
Peep, Chirp, Peep!

The whole world
has something to say.
You just have to listen
in a listening way.

 Listen to the poem.
Repeat the sound words.

 Compare these sound words to those
you have read about this week.

 Talk about what it means to listen
in a "listening way."

Quick Tip

To talk about sounds
we can say:

The sound a ____
makes is ____.

The ____ makes a
(quiet, loud) sound.

What I Know Now

Think about the texts you read this week.

The texts tell about

_____

_____

_____

_____

 Think about what you learned this week.
What else would you like to learn?
Talk about your ideas.

 Share one thing you learned
about fiction stories.

Talk About It

Talk about the place in the photo.

 Draw a place where you go in your neighborhood.

 Label your drawing.

This place is

Trg

Tetra Images/Brand X Pictures/Getty Images

 Retell the story.

 Write about the story.

The setting of this story is

_____

- -

_____

Text Evidence

Page

An interesting place the dog goes is

_____

- -

_____

Text Evidence

Page

- -

_____

Talk about where you would take a pet in your neighborhood.

 Draw and **write** about it.

I would take my pet to

_____

- -

_____

Fiction is a made-up story that has characters.

 Listen to part of the story.

 Talk about the most important character.

 Write a detail about the character.

This character

_____

- - - - - - - - - - - - - - - - - - - -

_____

- - - - - - - - - - - - - - - - - - - -

_____

Draw the character and
the detail you wrote about.

Listen to pages 5–9.
Which character is telling the story?

Draw and **write** about this character
and what it wants.

I want

Look at pages 14–15.

 Talk about why the dog likes to say hello. How does the illustrator show this?

 Draw what the illustrator shows.

Find Text Evidence

Read to find out about the visit to see Nan.

Circle the word **go**.

We Go to See Nan

Cam and I go to see Nan.

Find Text Evidence

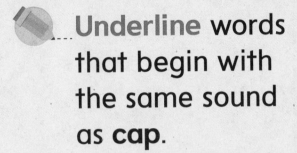

Underline words that begin with the same sound as **cap**.

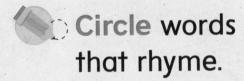

Circle words that rhyme.

Cam can pat the cat.

We can see the .

book

Shared Read

 **Find Text Evidence**

Circle who can sit on pages 72–73.

Retell the story. Use the words and pictures to help you.

Cam can go and sit.

The cat and I go and sit.

Paired Selection

Look at the map and the map key. How can these tools help us to learn about neighborhood places?

Talk about the pictures in the map key.

Draw a line from each picture on the map key to the place on the map.

Quick Tip

Each picture in the **map key** shows the matching place on the **map**.

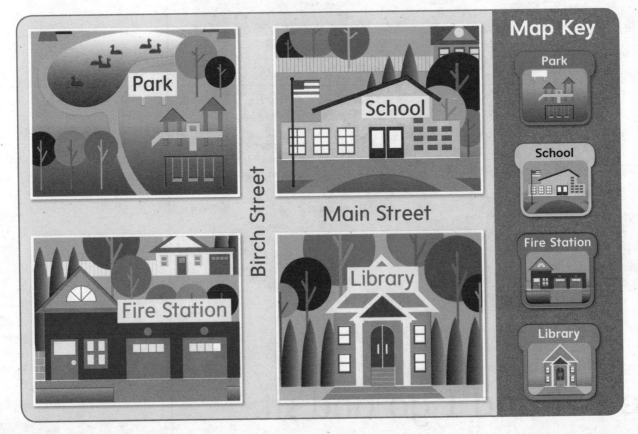

Park

School

Fire Station

Library

Birch Street

Main Street

Map Key

Park

School

Fire Station

Library

Talk about the places on the map.

 Draw and **write** about what people do in one of the places.

Talk About It

What does the map tell you about the neighborhood? How does the map key help you to use the map?

Find Text Evidence

 Read to find out where the girl and her mom can go.

 Think about what they can do at the library. Make a picture in your mind.

Can We Go?

Can we go to the  ?

library

Shared Read

🔍 **Find Text Evidence**

📝 **Underline** words that begin with the same sound as **cap**.

📝 **Circle** how the girl and her mom can go to the library.

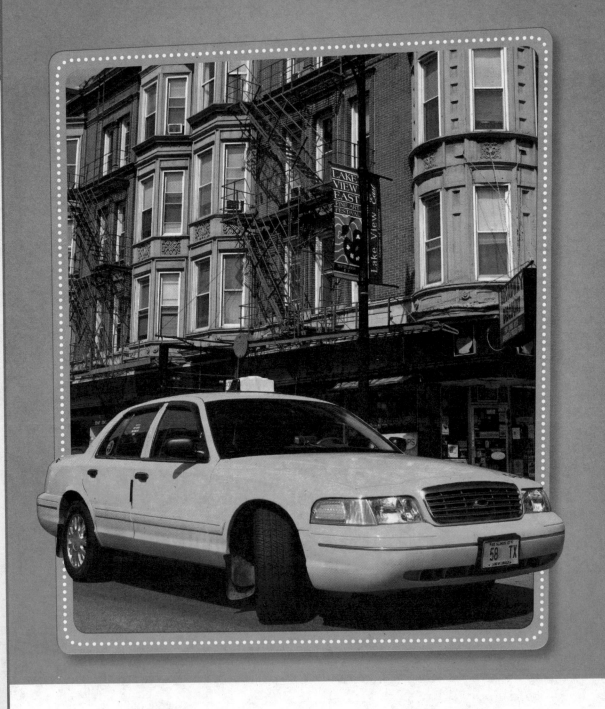

We can go in a .

taxi

Can we go to the ?
market

Shared Read

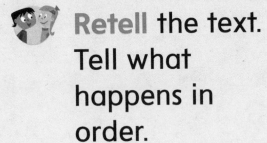 **Circle** the word **go**.

Retell the text. Tell what happens in order.

We can go in a .

bus

We can go, go, go!

Places in School

Step 1 **Talk** about the places in your school. Choose one place to learn about.

Step 2 **Write** a question about this place.

_____

- -

_____

_____

- -

_____

Step 3 **Visit** the place you picked. Ask the people there your question.

Step 4 Draw and write about what you learned.

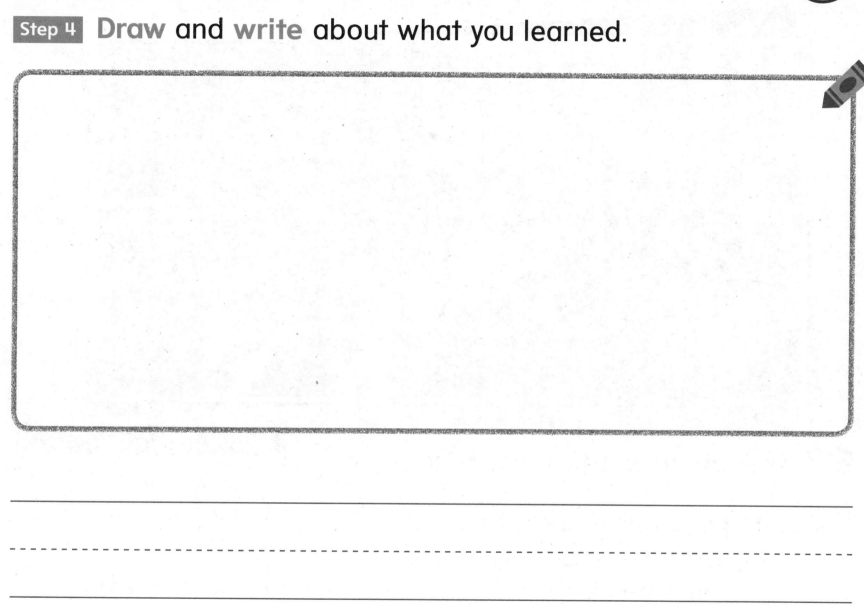

Step 5 Choose a good way to present your work.

 Talk about this farmers' market.

 Compare this market to other neighborhood places you read about this week.

Quick Tip

To talk about farmers' markets we can say:

Farmers' markets have fresh ____.

We can buy ____.

What I Know Now

Think about the texts you read this week.

The texts tell about

_____

- - - - - - - - - - - - - - - - -

_____

- - - - - - - - - - - - - - - - -

_____

 Think about what you learned this week.
What else would you like to learn?
Talk about your ideas.

 Share one thing you learned
about fiction stories.

My Sound-Spellings

Aa
a
apple

Bb
b
bat

Cc
c ck k
camel

Dd
d
dolphin

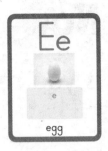

Ee
e
egg

Ff
f
fire

Gg
g
guitar

Hh
h_
hippo

Ii
i
insect

Jj
j
jump

Kk
c k ck
koala

Ll
l
lemon

Mm
m
map

Nn
n
nest

Oo
o
octopus

Pp
p
piano

Qq
qu_
queen

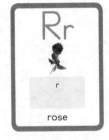

Rr
r
rose

Ss
s
sun

Tt
t
turtle

Uu
u
umbrella

Vv
v
volcano

Ww
w_
window

Xx
x
box

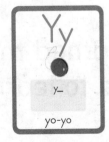

Yy
y_
yo-yo

Zz
z
_s
zipper

Credits: (apple) Stockdisc/PunchStock; (bat) Radlund & Associates/Artville/Getty Images; (camel) Photodisc/Getty Images; (dolphin) imagebroker/Alamy; (egg) Pixtal/age fotostock; (fire) Comstock Images/Alamy; (guitar) Jules Frazier/Getty Images; (hippo) Michele Burgess/Corbis; (insect) Photodisc/Getty Images; (jump) Rubberball Productions/Getty Images; (koala) Al Franklin/Corbis; (lemon) C Squared Studios/Getty Images; (map) McGraw-Hill Education; (nest) Siede Preis/Photodisc/Getty Images; (octopus) Photographers Choice RF/SuperStock; (piano) Photo Spin/Getty Images; (queen) Joshua Ets-Hokin/Photodisc/Getty Images; (rose) Steve Cole/Photodisc/Getty Images; (sun) 97/E+/Getty Images; (turtle) Ingram Publishing/Fotosearch; (umbrella) Stockbyte/PunchStock; (volcano) Westend61/Getty Images; (window) Photodisc/Getty Images; (box) C Squared Studios/Getty Images; (yo-yo) D. Hurst/Alamy; (zipper) ImageState/Alamy